FALL IN *Love* WITH YOURSELF

THE ART OF LOVING YOU

RHONDA THOMAS-BOOTHE

©2026 Copyright Rhonda Thomas-Boothe
All Rights Reserved
Printed in the United States of America

Hardback ISBN: 979-8-9947955-0-7
Paperback: 979-8-9947955-1-4
Digital: 979-8-9947955-2-1
Library of Congress Control Number: 2026909220

Book design: Emery McClendon
Photo credit back cover of the book: Cyrie Melody
Inside pictures: Aleyana Boothe
Editor: Karen A. Sims-Harrell, Twisted Threads LLC
Publisher: B&B Mind Over Matter Coaching & Mentoring LLC.

DEDICATION

This book is dedicated to my mothers, Genevieve and Janice, whose love and strength gave me life and purpose.

To my husband, who recognized that my life was worth saving and stood by me through every rise and fall.

To my sister circle, who embraced me, nurtured my growth, encouraged me to keep reaching for the stars, and allowed me to share my culture with pride.

To my mentor and friend, Dr. Tiffani Warren, thank you for inspiring me to serve with purpose, not only in my community but also in my home and in my own heart.

To the TRIBE, for the invaluable experiences, opportunities, and spaces you have shared with me.

To my best friend, thank you for your steady presence and for grounding me when my mind was clouded and my heart was uncertain.

And to my children, for loving me through every stage of my journey and allowing me to confront my mental health challenges without shame.

A special thank you to my self publishing mentor Veronica Moore, for all her patience and guidance through the process.

Finally, thank you to all my family, friends, and mentors who helped me along my journey. I love you ALL!

This book is for all those who have ever been told they were not enough—not good enough, not beautiful enough, not intelligent enough, or not loved enough.

Know that you are, and have always been, more than enough and loved!

Before you start your journey, take a deep inhale and then exhale!!

CONTENTS

A LETTER TO THE LOVE THAT WAS NOT...

Dear Oxycodone,

I wish I had never met you! You came into my life when pain ruled my days and nights. I was lost, and I was happy you were here. At first, you were relief, an answer, and a soft, calming voice that quieted the agony I was experiencing. You wrapped yourself around my pain and gave me rest.

Rest that I needed during the pain. My God, Oxycodone, you delivered!!!

Then one day, along the way, you did not just take the pain, you took the edge off everything, you numbed more than my body. What did you do to me? You silenced my thoughts, my spirit was now gone, and all I could see was darkness and despair. I was no longer myself but a shell of my true self, now fighting to get out of the darkness. The darkness that would keep me hostage to the noises in my head. What did you do to me? Oxycodone, you are not healing. You took more than what you gave me.

I loved you and needed more of you, and you did not disappoint me. Oxycodone, it was not easy to get rid of you! I wanted you, but others knew you were wrong for me. It was not easy, and I knew I could no longer lie or hide you from them. I stopped protecting you, and I chose to protect myself!

Every day without you was an act of courage that I had to take. I learned to live and love myself without you. The pain was strong, but my mind and will were stronger. Now, there are no more illusions! The darkness is now light, hate is now love built from within, and what once broke me now builds me. Once you were a chapter, but you did not get to be the end of my story.
Thank you because I got to say goodbye!!
Sincerely,

I survived, and I learned to love all of me.

UNDERSTANDING SELF-LOVE

Self-love is more than just a concept; it is a transformative practice that enhances every aspect of life. In this book, I will guide you through actionable steps to build a loving, nurturing, respectful, and free-from-judgment relationship with yourself, which will also improve your mental well-being.

Understanding self-love is the foundation of a healthy, balanced life. It is a process of cultivating a deep, unconditional love and acceptance for yourself, your flaws, your strengths, and everything in between. It is not about arrogance or selfishness, but rather about cultivating a compassionate and respectful relationship with who you are deep down in your core.

While self-love is about valuing yourself, it is different from narcissism. Narcissism is an excessive focus on oneself, often at the expense of others. This behavior can result in mental health issues like anxiety and depression, and in some cases long term truama. Self-love, on the other hand, is about having a healthy sense of self-worth while still valuing and respecting others. It is about nurturing yourself so you can be a better person for both yourself and the people around you.

Here is a deeper dive into what self-love really means:

At its core, self-love means accepting yourself without judgment. This involves embracing both your strengths and weaknesses, as well as your successes and failures. It means loving yourself through both your flaws and your perfections, acknowledging that you are worthy just as you are, without needing to change to meet others' expectations or societal standards.

Self-love is a practice of showing yourself compassion, especially when things are not going as planned. It is being gentle when you make mistakes or face challenges, instead of being harsh or critical. You treat yourself with the same kindness that you would offer to a friend who is struggling.

One key aspect of self-love is setting boundaries, knowing when to say no, when to step back, and when to protect your time and energy. Setting healthy boundaries is an act of self-respect, and it helps maintain your emotional, mental, and physical well-being. It is about recognizing your needs and making choices that honor them.

To truly practice self-love, you must be aware of your thoughts, feelings, and actions. Self-awareness helps you recognize when you are being too hard on yourself or when you are not prioritizing your needs. It is about being aware of your emotions and how they impact your behavior and decisions. This awareness creates the space for positive change and growth.

Prioritizing your well-being is an essential part of self-love. This does not mean neglecting others but rather recognizing that your happiness and mental health are as important as anyone else's. Whether it is taking time for self-care, resting when you need it, or pursuing passions or projects that nourish your soul. Prioritizing yourself is key to living a balanced, fulfilling life.

Self-love is a lifelong journey of growth, and it means continuously learning, evolving, and healing from past wounds. Loving yourself does not mean you will never face struggles or setbacks; it means honoring your resilience and capacity to heal. You permit yourself to grow at your own pace, without judgment or pressure.

In difficult moments, self-love is about being your own source of support. Instead of relying on external validation to feel worthy, you learn to validate and encourage yourself. This does not mean you should isolate yourself from others, but it is about strengthening your own inner voice, becoming your own cheerleader, and trusting that you are enough, even in moments of doubt.

True self-love is unconditional. It is not based on achieving certain things or meeting particular standards. It is the practice of loving yourself without expecting anything in return or placing conditions on your worth. You are worthy simply because you exist, and you treat yourself with respect regardless of your achievements or shortcomings.

The more you love and care for yourself, the more you can offer love and kindness to others. Self-love creates a foundation for healthy, balanced relationships because you can set boundaries, communicate openly, and express yourself authentically. When you value yourself, you are less likely to tolerate unhealthy dynamics and more likely to attract positive and respectful relationships.

Self-love is not a destination but a continual practice. There may be days when it is harder to love yourself, and that is okay. It is about understanding that showing up for yourself consistently, even on tough days. Over time, self-love becomes a natural part of who you are, and it helps to strengthen your ability to face challenges with grace and resilience.

When you practice self-love, you step into your power. You stop seeking external validation or approval because you know your worth. Self-love enables you to make decisions that align with your values, and it gives you the confidence to pursue your dreams, regardless of the obstacles.

MINDFUL MOMENT: Balance and boundaries are areas where individuals often struggle, particularly when care is not prioritized for oneself and instead placed on others. It creates a pattern where 'no' is not accepted.

This is the time to practice self-awareness!

Define your understanding
of Self Love

Define your understanding
of Self Love

CHAPTER ONE

WHY SELF-LOVE MATTERS

If you had told my younger self that self-care matters, I would have asked why and to whom? If asked today, I could give you many reasons why it matters more than ever. This is because we live in a world where we seek validation from individuals behind screens on social media, and every moment we experience depends on a stranger's reaction. Then others define beauty and uniqueness as not part of societal norms. We are constantly judging ourselves, striving to reshape our bodies even when that pursuit places our well-being at risk.

Ultimately, we hold on to negative friendships and relationships like a lifeline, which psychologically destroys our emotional and mental health. Even when these connections drain us, they provide a sense of identity, routine, or validation that can be difficult to release. Over time, this attachment distorts our self-perception, and we begin to normalize disrespect, minimize harm, and internalize criticism as truth. The longer we remain, the more our emotional and mental health deteriorates, leaving us anxious, depleted, and disconnected from our own needs. Letting go becomes not an act of loss, but an essential step toward self-preservation and healing.

Hence, we search for love in all the wrong places, within the wrong spaces and the wrong people, hoping to fill the emptiness left by unhealed wounds. Instead of finding connection, we often encounter cycles of disappointment that reinforce our fears and self-doubt. In mistaking familiarity for love, we settle for relationships that mirror our pain rather than nurture our growth, delaying the healing we so deeply need.

The philosophy of self-love teaches us that, to love others truly, we must first love ourselves. Without a solid foundation of self-love, it becomes difficult to build meaningful, healthy relationships. When you learn to value yourself, you set the standard for how others should treat you. Self-love is not only about improving the relationship with yourself but also about enriching your interactions with the world around you.

Additionally, self-love encourages personal growth and authenticity. It helps you live life according to your true values, rather than being shaped by others' expectations. When you love yourself, you are free to pursue your passions, take risks, and embrace your individuality without fear of judgment. When you practice self-love, you reduce self-criticism and increase self-esteem, leading to greater mental well-being.

Loving yourself helps you trust your abilities and believe in your potential, which naturally leads to higher confidence. Self-love motivates you to take better care of your body and mind, whether it is through exercise, eating well, or getting adequate rest. It helps you manage stress more effectively by encouraging you to take breaks, set boundaries, and release unnecessary pressure.

How to Start Understanding Self-Love:

- Reflect on your self-talk: Start by observing how you speak to yourself. Is it gentle, supportive, and kind? Or is it critical? Shifting from negative self-talk to positive affirmations is a powerful way to nurture self-love.

- Make time for yourself: Are you what you really want to do? Carve out time each day for activities that recharge you, whether that is reading, taking a walk, or simply resting. This shows you that you are worth the time and care.

- Practice mindfulness: Mindfulness helps you connect with the present moment and allows you to treat yourself with greater compassion. Through mindful practices such as meditation and breathing exercises, you can cultivate a deeper connection with yourself.

MINDFUL MOMENT: Self-love is a journey of growth, acceptance, and kindness. It is about respecting your individuality and acknowledging your worth without needing external validation. How do you currently show yourself love, and are there areas you would like to explore more?

Why is it Important to Embrace Self-Love?

Why is it Important to Embrace Self-Love?

Why is it Important to Embrace Self-Love?

CHAPTER TWO

RECOGNIZING YOUR WORTH

For many years, I searched for love that was rooted in others, material things, or anything that would bring me joy. All those things made me feel good for a brief time, but it did not last. The dopamine cycle would start and repeat! My worth was measured by loving others so they could love me back more, by the beautiful things that would put a temporary smile on my face, which would quickly fade.

One day, I had to face a difficult question when I heard a voice asking me, "what was I searching for?" This, coupled with being told for years that I was not worth "what paddy shot at" (Barbadian expression meaning worthless). This feeling of worthlessness became a quiet battle, because deep down, I knew I was more than what I believed myself to be.

Eventually, my mental space was where I had to constantly prove myself to others. I remember working for a non-profit in New York City, where I held the position of a database manager. I was certified to manage the database program, and I was confident in my skills. It was a job that I looked forward to going to, and one might say I loved my job. However, when the new Executive Director came on board, he wanted to "clean house". Every week, he found a reason why I should not be sitting in my position. He questioned every training under the sun that I had completed. His means to make me feel like I did not belong would not stop.

In the last meeting I had with him, he told me that I did not have a college degree, and I was not qualified for the job. Although I had already invested 10 years of work experience, training, and certifications, I was still not good enough.

His words cut deep, not because they were true but because of how easy one's worth can be diminished by another person in a leadership role.

Instead of internalizing the opinions of others or

blaming yourself for how they perceive you, take a step back and realign your thoughts and actions. I realized that one of my most deferred dreams was earning a college degree. For years, I had tucked that desire away, convincing myself it was impractical or no longer meant for me. Yet the dream never disappeared; it lingered quietly, resurfacing whenever I questioned my purpose or imagined a different future. Acknowledging it felt both daunting and liberating, as if I were finally permitting myself to want more and to believe that growth was still possible.

In 2017, I began my college journey, committing myself with the encouragement of my sister circle and mentor to seven years of learning that culminated in earning an Associate's, a Bachelor's, and a Master's degree. While those achievements strengthened my academic credentials, they did something far greater, they reshaped how I saw myself. When I walk into a room now, I know who I am and understand the perseverance it took to get to this point. I no longer ask for permission to belong. The door is open, and I take my seat at the table!

Self-worth is incredibly important! It is a deep understanding that you are valuable and deserving of love, respect, and care simply because you exist. Your self-worth is not determined by what others think, or by your achievements, but by the inherent value you have simply by being you. Self-worth can be nurtured and strengthened over time through self-compassion, self-reflection, and healthy boundaries.

INTRINSIC VALUE: You are worthy of love and respect simply because you exist.

Focusing on your strengths and qualities fosters self-esteem and helps you appreciate who you truly are.

Embrace 1: Understand Your Value

- Reflect on your strengths, accomplishments, and unique qualities.
- Write down three things you are proud of about yourself every day.
- Practice daily affirmations that remind you of your value: "I am worthy of love and respect."

Embrace 2: Let Go of Comparison

- Stop comparing yourself to others and understand that your journey is unique.
- Practice gratitude for your individual qualities instead of feeling "less than" others.

Embrace 3: You are Unique

- Every road travelled is different, with various trials and tribulations. When you walk the rocky road, remember you will gradually arrive at the paved road.

- Give yourself some grace because the journey is yours and no one else's.

MINDFUL MOMENT: There comes a moment when you stop seeking validation in places that you never saw clearly. When you no longer solicit love, approval, or space in someone else's world. This will be the result of something within you quietly and powerfully awakened. You were never too much. You were never not enough! You were simply in rooms that could not hold your light. Your worth is not measured by who stays, who claps, or who chooses you. Your worth is measured by the way you choose yourself again and again, with soft hands and steady faith. Once you are awakened, you begin to walk differently. You speak your truth without shrinking. You stop chasing and start becoming. And suddenly, everything changes because when you know your worth, you stop asking others to set the price and set your own price.

How do you understand and acknowledge your worth?

How do you understand and acknowledge your worth?

CHAPTER THREE:

CULTIVATING COMPASSION FOR YOURSELF

We often hear the word compassion and think of others, but what about showing compassion for yourself? Throughout my young adult life, I did not realize that the pain I was experiencing along with depression was a signal for me to prioritize my well-being. Instead, I saw it as an imperfection, and I considered myself a failure. This realization led me down a dark and destructive path—one that forced me to confront addiction and the pain I caused others. Facing those truths became the beginning of a long, difficult journey toward accountability, healing, and the cultivation of genuine compassion. I cannot count how many times I pushed myself beyond the point of breaking, believing that pain was proof of strength and that endurance meant worthiness.

During my studies, I explored religions of the world for a class in Philosophy. I was drawn to Buddhism and the Four Noble Truths, which forms the foundation of this religion. The truths are the process of suffering, Dukkha, which was the experience, Samudaya, attachment to craving, and Nirodha is the process of freeing oneself from what one craves. Magga outlines the ethics and mental practices that stop craving and promote freedom. Siddhartha Gautama was the founder of Buddhism, and instead of sitting on the throne to become a powerful King, he chose to live outside the palace to understand and experience life suffering. His concept was that suffering is in the structure of life, and to gain freedom, you need to understand that suffering is unavoidable. Only then will you become enlightened through your own understanding of who you are and connect to a deeper sense of your strength.

You might be thinking now, why would you look at suffering as something positive? Some of us know that when you fall, the next step is to rise. I was diagnosed with migraines and could not understand the pain, all I knew was that I needed the pain to stop. I would be lost in my thoughts of walking in front of a bus or truck to make the pain stop. I would ask God to let me sleep and not wake up because I did not want to feel the pain. My thoughts were dark, and as the pain intensified, my thoughts got darker. I was in constant pain, and the only way out I thought was to take my own life. I was suffering internally, and I wanted the noises and the pain to stop.

I knew the pills were a temporary fix, but they took the pain away for a short time. Some days I took the pills, and there was no pain, until I could not stop. I had to go through not having the prescribed drugs (my life preserver) to cope with the underlying issue and to remove the craving, even though it was not done by choice. For me, taking the journey to a freedom that was lost was not pleasant. Eventually, in the process, there was a turning point through transformation and grace. I had to learn to forgive myself, a lesson that did not come easily.

Every time I faltered or fell, I reminded myself that mistakes were not proof of failure but opportunities for growth. Instead of harsh judgment, I met each misstep with compassion, slowly cultivating a gentleness toward myself I had never allowed before. It was in these moments of patience and understanding that I began to heal and recognize my own resilience.

Cultivating compassion for yourself is about learning to treat yourself with the same kindness, care, and understanding that you would offer to a loved one. It is the practice of recognizing that you, just like everyone else, are deserving of love and empathy, especially when things are not perfect. This doorway is all about replacing self-criticism with compassion, embracing your flaws, and giving yourself the grace to grow without judgment. Cultivating compassion for yourself is a powerful tool because it creates a foundation of emotional resilience. It allows you to bounce back from challenges with a sense of self-worth that is not dependent on external validation or perfection. When you approach yourself with kindness, you build trust in your ability to handle difficult situations without self-blame. You begin to see that mistakes are growth opportunities, and that your imperfections are simply part of being human.

Self-compassion does not mean avoiding

responsibility or excusing harmful behavior. It means treating yourself with care and kindness even when you slip up and using those moments as stepping-stones toward becoming your best self. It helps you develop a more loving and nurturing relationship with yourself, ultimately leading to a happier, more fulfilled life.

Embrace 1: Practice Self-Forgiveness

- Letting Go of Guilt: We all make mistakes, but self-compassion means acknowledging those mistakes and forgiving ourselves rather than holding onto guilt. Holding onto past failures only prevents us from moving forward. By forgiving yourself, you release emotional burdens and give yourself space to heal and grow.
- Acknowledge past mistakes and forgive yourself. Write a letter to your past self, offering compassion and understanding.
- Let go of guilt by accepting that everyone makes mistakes and that it is a part of growth.

Embrace 2: Speak to Yourself Kindly

- Shift your inner dialogue and replace self-criticism with kindness. Often, we are our harshest critics. When you make a mistake or face a challenge, it is easy to fall into negative self-talk like, "I'm not good enough" or "I always mess things up."

- Cultivating compassion means recognizing those moments of self-criticism and replacing them with kindness. Treat yourself like you would treat a friend who is struggling.

SOUL WORK: *Next time you find yourself being critical, pause and ask yourself: "What would I say to a friend in this situation?" Respond to yourself with the same encouragement and empathy you would offer to someone you care about.*

Embrace 3. Use Self-Kindness in Moments of Struggle

- Comfort Yourself: When you are feeling down or going through a tough time, it is important to comfort yourself rather than beating yourself up for not handling things better.
- Show yourself the same kindness you would show to a close friend or loved one.

SOUL WORK: *In moments of struggle, place your hand over your heart, take a few deep breaths, and say some-*

thing kind to yourself like, "It's okay to feel this way," or "I am doing the best I can."

Embrace 4. Be Mindful of Your Emotions

- Mindful Self-Compassion: When you are feeling hurt, angry, sad, or anxious, rather than suppressing or ignoring these emotions, practice being mindful of them. Recognize the emotion, accept it without judgment, and allow it to pass naturally.

- Self-compassion is about accepting your emotions without being overly critical of yourself for feeling them.

SOUL WORK: *Practice a mindfulness practice where you observe your emotions without judgment. For example, if you are feeling anxious, simply notice the sensation in your body and the thoughts that arise. Do not try to push them away. Acknowledge that it is okay to feel that way and that your emotions are valid.*

Explain how you define compassion and nurture
kindness towards yourself.

Explain how you define compassion and nurture
kindness towards yourself.

CHAPTER FOUR

SETTING BOUNDARIES FOR SELF-RESPECT

At some point, you must come to the realization that you matter. You can stop saying yes to every demand, request, plea, and suggestion. Eventually, your body battery will become completely drained. This is a result of attending every social gathering and consistently showing up, which eventually takes a toll. I wish I could have told my forty-something self, when I was lying in the hospital, to stop trying to do it all. I was praying to God as the arteries in my heart were closing, and the doctors and nurses were trying every medical option to keep me stable. I had seen all this medical stuff on TV, but never would I have thought I would see myself in a medical crisis. Have you ever noticed that when we are at our lowest or in sickness, we call on God and start the bargaining process? I promised him that I would rest and would give up all the extra meetings and events that were not productive if he granted me life.

When we turn to God at our lowest, we tap into a kind of spiritual wellness that nourishes and restores the whole of our being. It is in those moments of surrender when we feel weakest, most lost, or most broken that we find a source of strength beyond ourselves. Spiritual connection does not erase struggle, but it provides a grounding force, a reminder that we are not alone in pain or hurt. By leaning into that presence, we cultivate resilience, hope, and a deeper sense of peace that seeps into every aspect of our emotional and mental well-being.

Ultimately, I was stable, and the doctor reviewed my history and was shocked because I was doing everything right. All the requested tests came back normal. So how could this be? I saw this experience as an opportunity to reflect on my life and make the necessary mental and physical changes. I was honoring, loving, and giving others so much of my time, support, and energy, while I was drained. I had to make a change, which meant letting go of friends or family members who did not honor my boundaries, and creating space for me to continue my journey to self-love and wellness.

Setting boundaries for self-respect is about creating clear limits that honor your needs, emotions, and well-being, while protecting your energy from being drained or violated. Boundaries allow you to take care of yourself, maintain healthy relationships, and create a life where your needs are acknowledged and respected. When you set boundaries, you are not just protecting yourself from harmful situations, but you are also teaching others how to treat you. Healthy boundaries are a form of self-respect that allows you to prioritize your own emotional, mental, and physical health without guilt.

Before you can set boundaries, it is important to understand what you need and where your limits lie. This involves reflecting on situations where you feel uncomfortable, drained, or taken advantage of. Recognize what caused these feelings.

Embrace 1: Identify Your Boundaries

Boundaries can be set in many areas of your life, including:

- Physical Boundaries: Protecting your personal space, touch, and physical interactions with others.

- Emotional Boundaries: Protecting your feelings from being manipulated or drained by others.

- Mental Boundaries: Limiting unnecessary stress or negative thoughts from others or even your own mind.

- Time Boundaries: Setting limits on how much time you dedicate to certain tasks or people and giving yourself time for rest or personal activities.

SOUL WORK: *Review your relationships, work, and social obligations. Where do you feel over-extended or disrespected? Where are you giving more than you are receiving? These areas often require boundaries.*

- Reflect on situations where you feel drained or unappreciated. These are often signs that your boundaries need to be set or reinforced.

Embrace 2: Communicate Your Boundaries with Confidence

- Once you have identified the boundaries you

need, it is crucial to communicate them clearly and assertively. This is where many people struggle, fearing they will be seen as rude or selfish.

- Remember that your needs are just as important as anyone else's, and clearly stating your boundaries is a healthy, respectful act.

SOUL WORK: *Practice saying "no" in different scenarios.*

For example:

> *"I need to take care of myself right now, so I cannot commit to that."*
>
> *"I am unable to take on any additional work at the moment."*
>
> *"I need space right now, and I would appreciate it if you would respect that."*

Using "I" statements ("I need…," "I feel…") helps express your feelings without blaming others, making it easier for them to understand and respect your needs. Practice saying "no" when necessary, without guilt. Also, honor your own needs and give yourself permission to prioritize them.

It is not enough to just set boundaries once, but you must enforce them consistently to make them effective. This can be challenging, especially if people push back or try to disregard your limits. However, maintaining consistency is key to showing respect for yourself and ensuring that others respect you, too.

SOUL WORK: *If someone crosses a boundary, gently but firmly remind them of the limit. For example:*

> *"I have shared before that I need space in the evenings to rest and recharge. I would appreciate it if we could honor that."*
>
> *"I am unable to take on any more commitments right now. Please understand and respect that."*

It is also important to be prepared to follow through on consequences if someone repeatedly disregards your boundaries. For instance, if someone continuously ignores your time limits, you might need to say, *"I cannot continue with this conversation right now."*

Embrace 3. Set Emotional Boundaries with Yourself

- Often, we struggle with emotional boundaries because we tend to take on other people's emotions or interpret things too personally. Setting emotional boundaries with yourself means recognizing that other people's feelings and reactions are not your responsibility.

- You can empathize with others, but you do not need to carry their emotional burdens.

SOUL WORK: *Practice detaching from other people's emotions. If someone is upset or angry, remind yourself that their feelings are theirs, and you do not need to absorb them. Use affirmations like: "I am responsible for my own feelings, not others'."*

Embrace 4. Respect Your Boundaries and Prioritize Self-Care

- Setting boundaries is not just about protecting yourself from others; it is also about taking care of your own needs.

- Self-respect means respecting your own time, emotions, and energy.

- Once you set your boundaries, prioritize self-care as an essential part of maintaining them.

SOUL WORK: *After a busy day or week, take time to reflect and unwind. Use your boundaries to create space for activities that nurture your mind, body, and soul, like meditation, reading, or taking a walk. Let yourself rest without feeling guilty.*

Embrace 5. Accept That Some People May

Resist Your Boundaries

- Some people, especially those who are used to you being overly accommodating, may push back or struggle to understand your boundaries. This is normal, but it is important to stand firm in your choices.

- Respecting yourself and your boundaries may be uncomfortable for others, but it does not mean you should sacrifice your own well-being for their comfort.

SOUL WORK: *If someone resists your boundary, do not feel guilty. Simply reinforce your need with compassion: "I understand this might be difficult, but my decision to set this boundary is important for my well-being."*

Embrace 6. Know When to Let Go

- If someone consistently disrespects your boundaries, you will need to reassess the relationship.

- Healthy relationships, whether personal, professional, or familial, should be built on mutual respect. If a person continually disregards your limits, it might be necessary to let go or distance yourself for your own peace of mind.

SOUL WORK: *Reflect on relationships where boundaries*

are not being respected. Ask yourself if these relationships are adding value to your life or draining you. If necessary, decide to step back or even cut ties with those who consistently disrespect your boundaries.

MINDFUL MOMENT: Boundaries are a way to honor yourself and your needs. When you set and enforce boundaries, you teach others how to treat you, and you prioritize your own emotional, mental, and physical health. Boundaries also help you avoid burning out, protect your energy and build healthier, more balanced relationships. Setting boundaries is an act of self-respect, not selfishness. By establishing clear, healthy boundaries, you are choosing to show up for yourself and your well-being. That is essential to living a fulfilling and peaceful life.

List the boundaries you already have in place
and some new boundaries you need to establish.

List the boundaries you already have in place
and some new boundaries you need to establish.

CHAPTER FIVE:

EMBRACING IMPERFECTIONS

Embracing imperfections is challenging because you must first understand and accept them. Even with the best plastic surgery, there is always a flaw, and it is the reality we live in. Both men and women struggle with imperfections; the difference is that women are more likely to be vocal about them. I am sure that my husband has heard me complain numerous times about the fat I gained in my midsection after having three children via C-sections. I knew I could never wear a bikini, and I would always hide my body and judge myself as if it made me a horrible person. However, one day I expressed to my best friend that I was considering plastic surgery, and the response changed my mind. As my best friend stated, the body you have is a result of motherhood, and many women do not have that experience, so be proud of your body. It took some time for me to understand that my body carried the trauma of bearing and delivering children, and every flaw was a blessing in motherhood.

Did I stop trying to fix my imperfection? No, I still felt the need to explore one more option. I wondered if a scare tactic might finally convince me. I had already done research, and even watched a television show that highlighted the irreversible negative outcomes of plastic surgery. That was the signal I needed to avoid any procedure that could be harmful to my body.

I was introduced to Black Girls Run, a safe space for women of various backgrounds, ages, and sizes on their personal running journeys. Through this community, I learned to embrace running, which supported my wellness journey and helped reframed my thoughts to accept my imperfections.

Additionally, running strengthened my endurance for discomfort and became a valuable coping skill I used as part of my mental health check-in.

Our body is extraordinary, and it holds stories our

minds may try to forget. Stories written in tension, joy, love, and pain. Every experience, joyful or traumatic, leaves an imprint within us. The body becomes a living archive, recording what we have survived from childhood to adulthood. Sometimes we think we have moved on, yet our body tells a different story. A racing heartbeat at a sound or word that reminds us of the past. Shoulders tighten when we feel unsafe, and the stomach knots at the thought of a confrontation. This is not a weakness; this is memory. Our bodies simply remember what our minds have learned to silence.

The beauty of the body lies not only in its ability to remember, but also in its incredible capacity to heal. With care, patience, and awareness, we can teach our body that it is safe to release what it has been holding. We can rewrite the language of tension into one of trust and continuous healing.

Healing begins when we listen to our bodies with compassion rather than judgment. When we ask, *"What are you trying to tell me?"* instead of, *"Why are you like this?"* The ache, the fatigue, the anxiety are not enemies to conquer but messengers calling us home to ourselves.

To prevent trauma from shaping our daily lives, we

must nurture the connection between mind, body, and spirit. That means learning to ground ourselves when we feel overwhelmed, allowing emotions to flow rather than being buried, and creating practices that bring us back into balance, whether through breathwork, praying, movement, therapy, meditation, journaling, or stillness.

Every moment of self-care is a signal to your nervous system that you are safe now. Every gentle breath, every stretch, every act of presence tells your body: *You no longer have to fight to survive. You can rest. You can feel. You can touch. You can heal.*

Our body is not our enemy. It is our oldest companion, doing its best to protect us even when its language is painful. When we begin to love it, listen to it, and honor what we have endured, we unlock one of the purest forms of self-love: the kind that exists not just in our minds, but in every fiber of our very cells.

Real self-love does not begin when you feel flawless; it begins when you stop needing to be perfect. It is born in the quiet moments when you look in the mirror, see the cracks, the scars, the messiness, and choose to love yourself anyway. Remember that perfection was never the goal, and wholeness is the goal.

You are allowed to be a work in progress. To stumble, to fall, to heal slowly, and to feel unsure. Embracing your imperfection does not mean you give up on growth; it means you grow with grace.

It is saying:

I accept the parts of me that are still learning.

I am still in the stage of understanding. I forgive the moments I fell short.

I celebrate myself, not just when I shine, but even when I struggle.

This is self-love.

Unpolished. Unfiltered. Unapologetic!

Embrace 1. Accept Yourself as You Are

- Let go of the idea of "perfection," because it does not exist! Embrace flaws as part of your authentic self.
- Celebrate the things that make you different and unique.

Embrace 2. Accept Your Imperfections

- Recognize Your Humanity: Nobody is perfect. Part of self-compassion is accepting that you are not meant to be flawless.

- Your imperfections are what make you unique and real. Instead of focusing on what is "wrong" with you, embrace the things that make you different and see them as strengths.

SOUL WORK: *Make a list of the qualities you sometimes judge as imperfections (e.g., being emotional, struggling with certain tasks, physical traits). Now, reframe them in a positive light. For example, if you are a perfectionist, you might see that as your dedication to quality; if you feel too emotional, it might be because you deeply care about others.*

Embrace 3. Practice Radical Self-Acceptance

- Stand in front of the mirror and practice saying, "I love you just as you are."
- Focus on what makes you feel whole rather than seeking external validation.

MINDFUL MOMENT: Embracing your flaws is a rewarding gift to yourself. It allows you to shift from judgment to a place of compassion where peace is created. Flaws are reminders that you are human and even though you may feel messy and imperfect, you are indeed worthy!

List your flaws and explain why you believe
they are flaws? Are your daily activities
affected by these flaws?

List your flaws and explain why you believe they
are flaws? Are your daily activities affected by
these flaws?

CHAPTER SIX

BUILDING A HEALTHY RELATIONSHIP WITH YOUR BODY

How many of us look in the mirror and hate what we see? How many of us cannot find the motivation to make one change? How many of us plan to start a new diet or plan to work out? How many of us never achieve the desired goal? How many of us then feel worse about ourselves?

I will tell you that you are not alone! We all know that exercise and eating right goes hand in hand. However, it took me a long time to realize that building a healthy lifestyle was more than just eating all the right foods.

I was a very selective eater, and being selective, I lacked certain nutrients that were necessary for my body. My energy level was off, I would cramp a lot, I could not focus as I should, and I would constantly feel tired. Thus, the reality of having to take a wide selection of supplements was too much for me. I knew a change had to be made, and I had to tell myself that change was good. There was also a quote that I would read every time I went to the gym, which was "if it does not challenge you, it does not change you." I took that quote and applied it to every challenge I faced.

Building a healthy relationship with your body is an ongoing process that involves nurturing both your physical and mental well-being. It is about developing self-awareness, self-compassion, and balance. From the time you wake up, the relationship with your body begins and continues until you lay your body to rest at night. Hence, how you go to bed is equally important to how you wake up in the morning.

This relationship does not differentiate between young or older individuals, because we all keep busy in varying ways, need to have a healthy diet, and the required amount of sleep each night for our bodies to repair themselves. Getting quality sleep is essential at every stage of life because it allows the body and mind to restore and recharge. For teens, sleep supports healthy growth, brain development, learning, and emotional regulation. While adults rely on sleep for focus, productivity, mood stability, and long-term health.

I struggle with having quality sleep. It is a journey I am still working on since my creativity sparks at night, and I tend to get lost in my thoughts and words. I also know that the next day, my body and mind must play catch-up. For many years, not getting the required amount of sleep caught up to me, and my health suffered. This is when I listened to the doctors and those in my circle and focused on rest, kindness to myself, and recovery.

Prioritizing healthy sleep habits can help people of all ages build stronger, healthier relationships with their bodies and minds.

Here are some key steps to help foster a positive relationship with your body:

Embrace 1: Nurture Your Body with Love

- Engage in activities that make your body feel strong and healthy, whether through movement, rest, or nourishing food.

- Stop criticizing your appearance. Focus on what your body allows you to do and how it carries you through life.

Embrace 2: Be Kind to Your Body

- Practice body positivity by celebrating your body for all that it is and all that it does for you.
- Engage in practices like yoga or mindful movement to connect with your body.

Embrace 3. Practice Self-Compassion

- Treat yourself with kindness rather than judgment. Recognize that your body is unique and beautiful, no matter its shape or size.
- Speak to yourself as you would a friend, avoid negative self-talk, and replace it with positive affirmations or gentle encouragement.

Embrace 4. Focus on What Your Body Can Do Not Just How It Looks

- Shift your focus from appearance to functionality. Appreciate your body's abilities, whether it is walking, dancing, lifting, or healing from an injury.

- Celebrate small achievements and progress.

Embrace 5. Nourish Your Body

- Eat a balanced and nutritious diet that fuels your body, rather than focusing on restrictive or fad diets. The goal is to nourish, not to be deprived of food.
- Listen to your body's hunger and fullness cues. Eat mindfully and avoid eating out of stress or boredom.

Embrace 6. Move Your Body in Ways That Feel Good

- Engage in physical activity that you enjoy, whether it is walking, yoga, hiking, swimming, dancing, or playing a sport.
- Do not exercise solely for weight loss. Focus on movement that makes you feel strong, energized, and mentally healthy.

Embrace 7. Prioritize Rest and Recovery

- Adequate sleep and rest are crucial for both physical and mental health. Make sure you are getting enough restorative sleep and taking breaks when needed.

- Listen to your body's signals when it needs rest, and avoid pushing yourself too hard, especially when you are feeling fatigued.

Embrace 8. Develop Mindfulness and Body Awareness

- Engage in activities like meditation, deep breathing, or yoga to develop mindfulness and a deeper connection with your body.
- This can help reduce stress, increase body awareness, and promote acceptance.

Embrace 9. Let Go of Perfectionism

- No one has a "perfect" body, and striving for perfection can be harmful. Learn to embrace imperfections and appreciate the unique qualities of your body.
- Understand that your worth is not defined by your appearance. Focus on what truly makes you feel good and healthy from the inside out.

Embrace 10. Surround Yourself with Supportive People

- Build relationships with people who lift you up

and encourage your journey to self-love. Avoid environments or people who promote body-shaming or unrealistic beauty standards.

- Share your feelings with trusted friends or a therapist if you struggle with body image or negative thoughts.

Embrace 11. Challenge Societal Standards of Beauty

- Recognize that societal standards of beauty are often unrealistic and damaging. Learn to reject harmful beauty norms and define beauty on your own terms.
- Seek out body-positive media and follow social media influencers and platforms that promote self-love and inclusivity.

Embrace 12. Seek Professional Support if Needed

- If you are struggling with body image issues, eating disorders, or other mental health concerns related to your body, it may be helpful to speak with a therapist, nutritionist, or other health professional.

- Therapy can offer tools to address underlying emotional issues that impact how you view your body.

MINDFUL MOMENT: Building a healthy relationship with your body is a journey. It takes time and patience, but every small step you take toward self-compassion, acceptance, and balance will help you develop a healthier mindset and a more positive connection to your body.

Track your meals and movement,
what you consumed, and how you felt.
What changes would you like to make?

Track your meals and movement,
what you consumed, and how you felt.
What changes would you like to make?

Track your meals and movement,
what you consumed, and how you felt.
What changes would you like to make?

CHAPTER SEVEN

PRIORITIZING YOUR MENTAL AND EMOTIONAL HEALTH

Loving yourself is not just about affirmations, bubble baths, or days off. It is about learning to protect the spaces within you that no one else can see. Your peace, your emotional balance, and your mental well-being are sacred parts of you. Only then, when you learn to prioritize them, do you begin to live from a place of wholeness rather than survival.

Your mind and emotions speak to you constantly. Anxiety whispers when you have taken on too much. Sadness signals when something has gone unhealed. Frustration reveals where your boundaries have been crossed. Self-love begins when you stop ignoring those messages and start listening.

Therefore, prioritizing your mental and emotional health is not something you do once, because it is a lifelong practice. There will be days when you feel strong and grounded, and others when you feel fragile and uncertain. Both are okay because they are a part of healing.

The workplace can often be one of the most challenging environments for maintaining mental and emotional well-being. For many, it is where we spend the majority of our waking hours, and the energy we expend there significantly affects how we feel both on the job and at home. While a healthy work environment can foster growth, creativity, and collaboration, a toxic workplace can have the opposite effect, eroding confidence, increasing stress, and even triggering anxiety and depression.

Toxic environments often manifest in the form of micromanagement, unrealistic expectations, favoritism, lack of recognition, poor communication, and interpersonal conflicts. Employees may feel undervalued, overworked, or unsupported. Over time, these factors accumulate, creating chronic stress that impacts mental clarity, emotional resilience, and overall health. It is not just about feeling frustrated, it is about experiencing physical and psychological consequences. Sleep disturbances, chronic fatigue, headaches, difficulty concentrating, and a constant sense of tension are common outcomes of prolonged exposure to workplace toxicity.

Moreover, the emotional toll can extend beyond the office, affecting relationships, self-esteem, and even one's sense of purpose. Many people begin

to internalize the negativity around them, blaming themselves for systemic issues or assuming that their struggles are personal failings. This self-blame can perpetuate cycles of anxiety, depression, and burnout.

Life often demands that we pause and take a clear look at the people and situations that weigh on us, draining our energy and clouding our thoughts. These negative influences do not always announce themselves, they creep into our routines, subtly shaping how we feel, react, and make decisions. By stopping to recognize them, we create space to set boundaries, reclaim our focus, and protect our mental and emotional well-being. It is not always easy, but acknowledging what hinders us is the first step toward creating a life that nurtures growth, peace, and clarity.

As I was completing my studies in 2023, I experienced some life-changing situations personally and professionally that were both tragic and toxic. First, I had to look at each situation and how it was impacting me. I also had to make a difficult decision: was I willing to take the path that included using Xanax, a medication designed to calm the central nervous system and ease anxiety? It was not a choice I took lightly. I had to weigh the potential relief it could bring against the reality of relying on a prescription drug, understanding both its benefits and its risks as I navigated my journey toward mental and emotional stability.

Having recovered from opioids misuse, I struggled with medicating myself or suffering in silence. So, I continued to use exercise, prayer, and balance as coping skills to address each situation in the workplace. Understanding that balance requires adopting healthy habits, such as eating well, exercising, engaging in positive conversations, getting enough sleep, and maintaining healthy relationships. Prioritizing your mental and emotional health is essential for overall well-being. Just as you care for your physical health, it is important to make time for nurturing your mind and emotions.

Recognizing what is and the impact of a toxic workplace is the first step toward reclaiming control. It requires pausing, reflecting, and evaluating which situations and relationships are draining your energy. Setting boundaries, seeking support, and cultivating healthy coping strategies are essential for protecting your mental health. By prioritizing your well-being, you not only survive the challenges of a toxic environment but also create the foundation to thrive, regardless of external circumstances.

Here are some strategies to help you prioritize your mental and emotional health:

Embrace 1. Recognize and Accept Your Emotions

- It is okay to feel a wide range of emotions, like happiness, sadness, anger, or anxiety. Accept your emotions without judgment, as they are natural parts of being human.
- Practice mindfulness to stay aware of how you are feeling and why. This helps you to respond to emotions in a healthy way rather than reacting impulsively.

Embrace 2. Develop Healthy Coping Mechanisms

- Life can be stressful, and developing healthy coping strategies is crucial for mental health. These can include deep breathing, journaling, meditation, or talking to a trusted friend.

- Avoid unhealthy coping skills like overworking, substance use, or emotional eating. Instead, lean into habits that support long-term emotional well-being.

Embrace 3. Establish Boundaries

- Protect your mental health by setting clear boundaries with work, relationships, and other obligations. It is okay to say "no" when something does not align with your priorities or when you need time for yourself.

- Respecting your personal boundaries helps maintain your energy and mental clarity.

Embrace 4. Build a Support System

- Surround yourself with supportive people who respect and understand you. Having a network of friends, family, or professionals who you can turn to during tough times can make a significant difference.

- Do not hesitate to seek professional help when needed. Therapists and counselors can provide valuable tools for coping with emotional struggles.

Embrace 5. Take Breaks and Practice Self-Care

- Regular breaks and self-care are vital to mental health. Take time each day to engage in activities that relax and recharge you, whether it is taking a walk, reading, or practicing yoga.
- Self-care can also involve engaging in hobbies you enjoy, getting a good night's sleep or simply taking a moment to pause and breathe.

Embrace 6. Challenge Negative Thought Patterns

- Pay attention to your thoughts, especially negative or self-critical ones. Practice reframing them by challenging their validity and replacing them with positive, realistic affirmations.
- Cognitive Behavioral Therapy (CBT) techniques can help you recognize and transform negative thought patterns.

Embrace 7. Cultivate a Positive Mindset

- Practice gratitude by regularly acknowledging the things you are grateful for. This shifts your focus from stressors to positive aspects of your life, which can improve your mood and outlook.
- Surround yourself with positivity, whether through uplifting media, books, or affirmations that help you stay optimistic.

Embrace 8. Exercise Regularly

- Physical activity is not only good for your body, but also for your mind. Regular exercise releases endorphins, the brain's "feel-good" chemicals, which can boost your mood and reduce anxiety.
- Find a form of exercise you enjoy, whether it is walking, yoga, dancing, or sports, to make it a sustainable part of your routine.

Embrace 9. Limit Stress and Practice Relaxation Techniques

- Chronic stress can have a major impact on mental health. Learn to manage stress through relaxation techniques like deep breathing, progressive muscle relaxation, or guided imagery.

- Make time for activities that reduce stress, such as spending time in nature, practicing mindfulness, or engaging in creative outlets like art or music.

Embrace 10. Be Kind to Yourself

- Practice self-compassion, especially during difficult times. It is normal to have bad days, and being too hard on yourself can make things worse.
- Treat yourself with the same kindness and understanding you would offer a friend.
- Accept that you cannot be perfect, and that it is okay to ask for help when you need it.

Embrace 11. Get Professional Help if Necessary

- If you are struggling with mental health issues such as anxiety, depression, or trauma, reaching out to a therapist or counselor is crucial. Professional support can provide valuable coping mechanisms and emotional relief.
- Therapy can help you understand and work through emotional challenges. In some cases, medication may be recommended for conditions like depression or anxiety.

Embrace 12. Develop a Routine

- A structured daily routine can provide stability and reduce feelings of overwhelm. Having a regular sleep schedule, consistent mealtimes, and dedicated time for work and relaxation helps promote emotional well-being.

- Incorporating positive activities into your routine, like exercise, reading, or hobbies, will create balance and reduce stress.

Embrace 13. Stay Connected with Nature

- Spending time outdoors can significantly improve mental and emotional health. Nature has a calming effect, reducing stress and improving mood.

- Even a few minutes outside each day, whether walking, gardening, or simply sitting in a park, can help recharge your mind.

Embrace 14. Limit Social Media and Technology Use

- Constant exposure to social media and digital distractions can lead to stress, comparison, and anxiety. Set boundaries around screen time and social media use.

- Focus on real-life connections and experiences rather than getting caught up in virtual comparisons or scrolling.

MINDFUL MOMENT: By consistently practicing these strategies, you can prioritize your mental and emotional health and cultivate a sense of balance and well-being. It is okay to seek help and take small steps toward making your mental health a priority. Incorporate mindfulness into your daily routine. Start with 5-10 minutes of meditation or deep breathing each day. Be present with your emotions and accept them as they come without judgment. Recognize that it is okay to ask for help, whether from a therapist, support group, or trusted friend. Take mental health breaks and do things that replenish your energy.

Log your emotions
throughout the day.

Log your emotions
throughout the day.

CHAPTER EIGHT

FOSTERING SELF-CONFIDENCE AND EMPOWERMENT

Was there something you could have done or said differently that would have had a more positive outcome?

Let us admit it! Some of us are born with it, while others have more work to do to find or build self-confidence. For me, stepping back into modeling at the age of 50 was a bright spark that fostered my self-confidence. Truth be told, confidence rises as you accept and love who you are, despite what others believe or think. When you shift from self-doubt to self-belief, you can manage whatever life throws at you. I used to speak to myself negatively because it was told to me, so if you never knew how to flip the switch, you could never foster self-confidence.

Education, along with the support of those who encouraged me, helped me realize I was more than enough. My mind, especially the hippocampus, had a lot of work to do relearning how to process experiences and replacing old, negative memories with new, positive ones. Each encouraging word and each small achievement became a building block in reshaping how I saw myself, proving that growth and healing were possible when nurtured with care and intention.

While in college, I came across positive psychology, and it immediately felt like it was speaking to my journey, affirming what I had been learning about myself and the power of mindset. It was a strength-based approach that looked at our positive qualities, happiness, social connections, and our overall satisfaction with our life. Understanding this approach allowed me to shift my focus toward the joy and purpose in my life. Instead of being consumed by fear, doubt, or external pressures, I noticed the small victories, the meaningful connections, and the moments that truly mattered. By consciously centering myself on what gave my life meaning, I discovered a deep sense of contentment and an empowering confidence that I had the strength to shape my own path.

Fostering self-confidence is not about being perfect or having all the answers; it is about learning to trust yourself, even when doubt creeps in. It permits you to make mistakes, to stumble, and to rise again without judgment. Every small step you take, every time you speak your truth or honor your own needs, strengthens that quiet, unshakable belief that you are enough. Confidence grows not from comparison or approval, but from recognizing your own worth and showing yourself the same kindness you would offer to someone you love.

Here are some embraces to build and maintain self-confidence and empowerment:

Embrace 1. Recognize Your Strengths and Achievements

- Reflect on your past successes and acknowledge your abilities. Celebrate even the small wins in your life and keep track of them to build your self-esteem.
- Take time to list your skills, talents, and positive

qualities. Remind yourself that you bring value to the world, regardless of external validation.

Embrace 2. Set Realistic Goals

- Set achievable and meaningful goals that align with your values and passions. Break them into smaller, manageable steps, and celebrate each milestone.
- Recognize that setbacks are a natural part of growth, and they do not diminish your worth. Learn from them and keep moving forward.

Embrace 3. Practice Self-Compassion

- Treat yourself with kindness and understanding, especially during moments of failure or difficulty. Instead of criticizing yourself, offer the same compassion you would give a friend.
- Let go of perfectionism. Understanding that making mistakes is part of the learning process, and those mistakes do not define your worth or abilities.

Embrace 4. Accept Your Uniqueness

- Celebrate what makes you different. Recognize

that your individuality is a source of strength and empowerment. Comparing yourself to others often leads to insecurity, but embracing your authentic self builds confidence.

- Focus on your personal journey rather than external expectations or standards.

Embrace 5. Challenge Negative Self-Talk

- Pay attention to the way you speak to yourself. Negative self-talk, such as "I can't do this" or "I'm not good enough," erodes self-confidence. Challenge these thoughts and replace them with positive affirmations.

- Practice re-framing negative beliefs. For example, instead of saying "I'm not good at this," try "I'm learning and improving every day."

Embrace 6. Take Care of Your Body and Mind

- Confidence is deeply connected to feeling good in your own skin. Engage in activities that nourish both your physical and mental health, such as regular exercise, healthy eating, sleep, and mindfulness.

- When you take care of yourself, it boosts your

energy and self-esteem, allowing you to approach life with a more empowered mindset.

Embrace 7. Step Outside Your Comfort Zone

- Taking on new challenges and stepping outside your comfort zone helps to grow your confidence. It may feel uncomfortable at first, but each experience teaches you resilience and strengthens your belief in yourself.
- Whether it is trying a new hobby, speaking in public, or standing up for yourself; embracing discomfort leads to personal growth.

Embrace 8. Build Healthy and Strong Relationships

- Surround yourself with people who support and uplift you. Positive, empowering relationships are key to building self-confidence.
- Limit time with those who bring negativity, criticism, or doubt into your life. Instead, nurture relationships that inspire growth and self-acceptance.

Embrace 9. Learn to Say "No"

- Setting boundaries is essential for self-empowerment.

Learn to say "no" when something does not align with your values or when you feel overwhelmed.

- Saying no gives you control over your time and energy, allowing you to focus on what truly matters to you without feeling guilty.

Embrace 10. Develop a Growth Mindset

- Embrace the idea that your abilities and intelligence can grow with effort and perseverance. A growth mindset allows you to see challenges as opportunities for learning and improvement, rather than as obstacles.
- This shift in thinking boosts confidence because you understand that success is not about being perfect, it is about progress and persistence.

Embrace 11. Practice Assertiveness

- Assertiveness is the ability to express your thoughts, feelings, and needs confidently and respectfully. Practice speaking up for yourself in both personal and professional settings.
- Whether you are expressing your opinions or standing up for your rights, assertiveness empowers you and reinforces your sense of self-worth.

Embrace 12. Visualize Success

- Visualization is a powerful tool for building confidence. Take time each day to mentally envision yourself succeeding in different areas of your life. This can help reduce anxiety and increase your belief in your abilities.

- Picture yourself achieving your goals, handling challenges with grace, and feeling proud of your accomplishments.

Embrace 13. Surround Yourself with Inspiration

- Read books, listen to podcasts, or follow people on social media who inspire you. Empowering stories, messages of resilience, and words of encouragement can help boost your own sense of confidence.

- Finding role models who share your values can show you what is possible and motivate you to keep moving forward.

Embrace 14. Accept Failure as Part of Growth

- Understand that failure is not a reflection of your worth. It is a part of the learning process. Instead of fearing failure, embrace it as a steppingstone toward growth.

- Every setback holds valuable lessons that contribute to your future success. Recognizing this empowers you to take risks and keep trying.

Embrace 15. Celebrate Yourself

- Take time to appreciate your journey. Reward yourself for your achievements and acknowledge your progress, no matter how small.
- Celebrating your wins, whether big or small, helps reinforce your belief in yourself and encourages you to keep going.

Embrace 16. Stay Persistent and Patient

- Confidence and empowerment do not happen overnight. It is a process that takes time and requires you to be patient with yourself.
- Stay consistent in working toward your goals and be kind to yourself along the way. Trust that every effort you make is contributing to your overall growth.

MINDFUL MOMENT: By actively incorporating these practices into your daily life, you can build a deep sense of self-confidence and empowerment. Remember, you have everything you need within you to succeed and thrive. The more you invest in yourself, the stronger and more confident you will become. Write down goals that are meaningful to you. Break them into small, achievable steps. Celebrate each small victory and remind yourself of your progress. Create a list of your personal strengths and read it aloud to yourself regularly. Challenge self-doubt by taking action toward your goals, even if it feels uncomfortable at first.

I challenge you to step out
of your comfort zone.

I challenge you to step out
of your comfort zone.

I challenge you to step out
of your comfort zone.

CHAPTER NINE

EMBRACING JOY AND FUN

On my journey, my oldest daughter was one of my inspirations for embracing joy in growth. I watched her research the different flowers that would help bees to produce different types of honey flavors and colors. She also researched the types of soil needed to start our small garden. The care and time that she took to grow our vegetables, and then harvest them, brought her so much joy. It is with that joy that I learned to stop and embrace the Joy Bloom.™

The Joy Bloom™ theory reveals that joy does not arrive at all at once, nor does it arrive from outside sources. Thus, it gradually blooms, taking root from within us, gently expanding as you nurture your relationship with yourself and foster intentional moments. Then, just like a flower, your joy blooms.

Therefore, to understand the concept of embracing joy, we must progress through stages of growth, which are represented by deeply lived experiences over time. Joy is rooted in the collection of moments that shape us, shared laughter, the relief after surviving something difficult, the warmth of being seen and understood. Each experience leaves a trace, and over time these traces gather into something bigger, richer, and more grounded. Embracing joy means letting yourself feel all of it, the messy, the beautiful, the unexpected, and realizing that joy grows not despite life's complexity, but because of it.

Joy Bloom™ Stages
The Seed: 🦋 Stage of Self Awareness

In this stage, there is a transformation where you become aware of yourself, your needs, wounds, desires, and dreams. It is also a stage of quiet and stillness, yet one of great power. In the stage of self-awareness, you must care for yourself.

The Soil: 🦋 Stage of Self-Compassion

Remember, you bloom best in the soil of kindness. Instead of criticizing yourself, you learn to speak gently and treat yourself with care and love. You learn to nurture compassion, creating emotional safety where joy can safely grow.

The Roots: 🦋 Stage of Boundaries & Worthiness

Plants and flowers cannot bloom without strong roots. These roots are your boundaries, your standards, and the belief that you are worthy of respect, rest, and love. The deeper the roots, the more grounded you become in who you are, and you build resilience for the difficult times. As a result, you begin to fill up with joy.

The Stem: 🦋 Stage of Daily Nourishment

Just like the role of the stem is to bring nourishment to a flower, joy needs daily sunlight, food for the soul, and consistent acts of self-love. Hence, sunlight on your skin, eating healthy, breathing deeply, moving your body, honoring your no, resting without guilt, and choosing what makes you come alive. These are the nutrients needed to produce and foster joy!

The Bloom: 🦋 Stage of Overflowing Joy

This is the moment you feel your own beauty and radiance. Joy does not come from perfection but alignment! You bloom when your outer life begins to reflect your inner growth. In this stage, you glow differently because you are finally growing for yourself!

The Garden: 🦋 Stage of Sharing the Joy

A bloom does not sit alone and stay pretty; it naturally spreads seeds. This is when your self-love inspires others, not because you try to fix or change them but because your joy permits them to bloom. The garden of joy attracts others to bloom bigger and brighter.

The Joy Bloom™ is powerful but not demanding. It honors healing as a living process that unfolds slowly and focuses on inner joy, rather than quick fixes. It turns self-love into something that is felt and practiced over time, rooting you in who you are becoming.

Joy is a garden you learn to maintain!

It is okay to foster joy in new relationships and experiences because social groups positively impact your life. Whether with a Sister Circle, A Tribe, Ladies that Lunch, Fitness or Run group, etc., it is imperative that we all enjoy life to the fullest. My mentor was the life of any gathering we had; she had an infectious laugh and a glow that lit up any room. She taught me that it did not matter what position one held, or how many tasks one had to do; it was important to take time to always laugh and have fun. She had already experienced all the stages and shared Joy with everyone in the sister circle, and those around her always left her presence smiling or laughing.

Embracing joy and fun is all about reconnecting with the lighter side of life, stepping away from stress, and allowing yourself to experience moments of happiness, laughter, and spontaneity. It is important to make time for joy because it nurtures your well-being, boosts your mood, and helps you feel more balanced and grounded.

Embrace 1. Make Time to Play

- Life does not have to be all about work and responsibilities. Carve out time for playful activities that bring you joy, whether it is playing a game, drawing, dancing, or just being silly.
- Try activities that make you feel lighthearted and free, this could be anything from going to a trampo-

line park to playing with a pet or jumping in puddles after a rainstorm.

- Even routine tasks can be made fun if you approach them with a lighthearted attitude. Sing while you clean, turn chores into a game, or make a playful challenge out of mundane tasks.
- Find ways to add a touch of humor or creativity to your daily routine, and you will notice how even the smallest moments can bring joy.

Embrace 2. Get Creative

- Creativity is a powerful way to access joy. Whether you are painting, writing, singing, crafting, or cooking, creativity allows you to express yourself and tap into a sense of fulfillment and fun.
- You do not have to be a professional artist, just the act of creating something new, with no pressure for perfection, can bring joy.

Embrace 3. Laugh Often

- Laughter is one of the best ways to lift your spirits and embrace fun. Watch a funny movie or show, listen to a comedy podcast, or simply spend time with people who make you laugh.

- Do not take life too seriously! Sometimes, the best moments are the spontaneous bursts of laughter that happen when you are with good company or doing something unexpected.

Embrace 4. Find Your Joy

- Joy does not always have to come from big events or elaborate plans. Often, the simplest things can bring immense happiness, enjoying a cup of coffee in the morning, listening to your favorite song, or feeling the sun on your face.
- Practice gratitude for these small, everyday joys. Focusing on the present moment helps you appreciate what's right in front of you.

Embrace 5. Surround Yourself with Positive Energy

- Spend time with people who uplift you, make you laugh, and share your sense of fun. Surrounding yourself with positive energy and like-minded individuals creates an atmosphere where joy is contagious.
- Do not be afraid to let go of relationships or environments that drain your energy and replace them with ones that inspire joy and fun.

Embrace 6. Let Go of Perfection

- Embrace imperfection and be open to messy, spontaneous experiences. Do not worry about getting everything "right." Joy often comes from the unexpected moments, not the planned ones.
- Allow yourself to be imperfect, make mistakes, and not take everything so seriously. This mindset frees you to experience more joy and fun.

Embrace 7. Try Something New

- New experiences often come with a sense of adventure and fun. Whether it is traveling to a new place, trying a new hobby, or simply stepping outside of your comfort zone, new activities can add excitement to your life.
- Challenge yourself to try something you have never done before. The excitement of newness can be invigorating.

Embrace 8. Do What Makes You Feel Alive

- Find activities that ignite your passion or bring a sense of thrill. This could be anything from hiking in nature, dancing, traveling, to doing something adventurous like riding roller coasters or trying out a new sport.

- Feeling alive and energized is a powerful way to experience fun and joy.

Embrace 9. Dance Because You Can

- Dancing is an amazing way to tap into your body's natural joy and energy. Whether you are in your living room, at a party, or in a park, allow yourself to let loose and enjoy the music.
- You do not need to be a skilled dancer to have fun, just move and express yourself in the moment.

Embrace 10. Go Outdoors

- Nature has a special way of helping us reconnect with ourselves and experience joy. Take a walk in the park, go for a hike, visit the beach, or simply sit outside and enjoy the beauty around you.
- Being outdoors can reduce stress, uplift your mood, and offer opportunities for spontaneous fun and adventure.

Embrace 11. Take a Pause from Technology

- Taking breaks from digital screens, whether it is stepping away from social media, email, or TV, can help you reconnect with yourself and the present moment. Disconnecting allows space for more natural, unplanned joy.

- Take a day or even just a few hours to be offline, and use that time to engage in a fun, offline activity that makes you feel good.

Embrace 12. Let Go of Worry and Fear

- Fun and joy thrive in an environment free from worry and fear.
- Practice letting go of anxiety by focusing on what is happening in the moment rather than stressing about what could go wrong.
- Embrace spontaneity and allow yourself to take risks, knowing that not everything has to be controlled or planned out for you to enjoy it.

Embrace 13. Enjoy Your Favorite Treats

- Sometimes, joy comes from simple pleasures like indulging in your favorite dessert, enjoying a relaxing bath, or having a lazy day watching movies.
- Take time to treat yourself without guilt, whether it is a special meal, a spa day, or just spending time

doing nothing. Enjoying life's little pleasures is a big part of embracing joy.

Embrace 14. Be Grateful

- Gratitude can amplify your sense of joy. When you experience a fun moment, take a moment to appreciate it, whether it is a shared laugh with friends or a spontaneous adventure.
- Practicing gratitude reminds you of the joy you already have and helps you embrace even more of it.

MINDFUL MOMENT: Embracing joy and fun is not about being carefree all the time, it is about giving yourself permission to enjoy life and celebrate the little moments. By intentionally carving out time for joy and incorporating playful activities into your routine, you can cultivate a more fun, vibrant, and fulfilling life.

Make time for hobbies and activities that make you feel good, things that bring you joy, without any need for validation. Rediscover the things you loved to do as a child, whether that is painting, playing, dancing, or exploring. Let go of the idea that you always need to be productive. Sometimes, joy and play are just as important as work.

List the things that bring you joy.

List the things that bring you joy.

List the things that bring you joy.

113

CHAPTER TEN:

STARS IN MY GARDEN

List the simple things you enjoy.

I have to say thank you to myself
for being alive.
It was a hard journey we're still on.
It will just take time.

But since we exist,
since we live,
we get to meet stars that have fallen to earth.
I know in my heart.
I am finally happy to be alive.

I just want to get lost in life.
Forget about time.
Happy we're here,
happy we exist,
happy our timelines have intertwined.
I could cry
knowing I'm alive
and living life along your side

Isn't it crazy how I didn't think
we'd speak again?
Isn't it wild
how consistently kind so many people can be?
The universe surprises and got a humor.
I'm thankful for what you don't know you did for
me.

So I'm happy I am alive.
I'll stay for the ride.
Continue to get to know me.

I just want to get lost in life.
Forget about time.
Happy I'm here,

happy I exist,
happy our timelines have intertwined.
I could cry
knowing I'm alive,
truly living life as I got to know you.

The longer I stayed alive,
I got to learn my parents' sides.
The longer I stayed alive,
I got to see my parents' smiles.
The longer I stay alive,
my siblings are turning out better than I am.
The longer I stay alive,
I am more and more grateful for the people I meet
in life.

I just want to get lost in life.
Forget about time.
Happy I am here,
happy I exist,
happy our timelines have intertwined.
I could cry
knowing I am alive,
truly living life as I got to know you and I.

I am building a garden.
Come visit me!
In this garden stay as long as you need.
Don't underestimate, I got my boundaries.
My little garden is only for me,
but I invite you to lay down,
stare at the sky now.
Experience life
as you are
Alive.

By Aleyana Boothe, 2025

Life is like a Garden

Aleyana Bee, 2024

CHAPTER ELEVEN

CREATING A SPACE FOR SELF-LOVE

Stepping away from my family to create the space that was needed took a lot for me as a mother, wife, friend, sister, and devoted person to my work and duties. I remember laying on the beach asking God to explain the need to be alone because I could not understand being away from my husband and kids without feeling like it was wrong. In that very moment, it was like hush and healing at the same time, all I heard was the sound of the waves, and each crash of the wave was a different sound. As I listened to the waves, a sense of calmness washed over me. My body loosened, my mind quieted, and for the first time in a long while, everything felt…. good. The rhythm of the ocean reminded me that stillness can heal, and that peace is often found in the simplest moments. This is spiritual wellness!

Every time I try to question why I needed space, I return to the answer I received on the beach in Barbados. The clarity of that moment, the sound of the waves, the warmth of the sun, and the quiet around me remain etched in my memory. It reminded me that sometimes, stepping away is not about running from life or avoiding responsibility; it is about giving yourself the room to breathe, reflect, and reconnect with who you truly are. That lesson has stayed with me, guiding me whenever I feel the pull of doubt or the weight of expectation. Hence, breaking away from the turmoil in your head allows you time for self-awareness and self-reflection, which allows you to make changes to become a better version of yourself.

Self-love knows no age, and cultivating a self-love ritual is a powerful way to nurture your mind, body, and spirit. By intentionally carving out time for yourself, you create space to listen, reflect, and honor your needs. These rituals strengthen self-awareness, deepen acceptance, and remind you that caring for yourself is not selfish, it is essential to living fully and authentically.

Here is a simple guide to creating a ritual that works for you:

Embrace 1. Set an Intention

- Start by defining what self-love means to you. Is it about relaxation? Confidence? Gratitude? Having a clear intention helps you stay focused and gives purpose to your ritual.

Embrace 2. Create a Dedicated Safe Space

- Choose a space where you feel safe, comfortable, and undisturbed. It can be a corner of your room, a cozy chair, or even outdoors. Then add personal touches like candles, soft lighting, or flowers to make the space inviting.

Embrace 3. Use Calming Elements

- Aromatherapy: Light a scented candle or use essential oils like lavender, rose, or sandalwood to create a calming atmosphere.
- Music: Play soothing music or listen to affirmations that uplift you.
- Touch: Treat yourself with some skincare or a relax-

ing bath with your favorite bath salts or oils. Gently massaging your body with a lotion or oil can be a deeply loving gesture.

Embrace 4. Practice Positive Affirmations and Gratitude

- Write or speak affirmations that focus on self-love and acceptance.

  "I am worthy of love and respect."
  "I honor and celebrate my uniqueness."
  "I embrace my flaws and know they make me whole."

- You can also practice gratitude by acknowledging things about yourself that bring you joy and gratitude. This could be your body, your talents, your kindness, or your resilience.

Embrace 5. Mindfulness and Meditation

- Take time to align yourself with mindfulness practice or meditation. Focus on your breath, grounding yourself in the present moment. You might also try loving-kindness meditation, where you repeat affirmations of self-compassion.

Embrace 6. Movement and Expression

- Engage in gentle movement, whether it is yoga, stretching, or simply dancing to music. This helps release tension and allows you to connect with your body lovingly.

Embrace 7. Journaling

- Write in a journal to reflect on your thoughts, emotions, and experiences. You can ask yourself questions like:

    What does self-love look like today?

    What are three things I love about myself right now?

    How can I show myself more love today?

Embrace 8. Nourishment

- Treat your body with love through healthy food, or whatever makes you feel nurtured. Whether it is sipping your favorite tea, enjoying a nutritious meal, or simply taking a moment to savor something you love, nourishing your body is a key part of self-love.

Embrace 9. Rest

- Ensure you include time for rest, whether it is a nap, deep sleep, or simply lying down and allowing yourself to relax. Rest is just as important as any other part of your self-care routine.

Embrace 10. Consistency in Self-love

- Make self-care a regular practice. Whether it is daily, weekly, or whenever you need it, consistency builds a deeper connection and reinforces the habit of self-love.
- The beauty of a self-love ritual is that it can be tailored to what feels best for you!

SOUL WORK: *Develop a daily routine of self-love and start each day with gratitude and affirmations. End each day by reflecting on what you did well and acknowledging your own efforts. Then create a Self-Love Toolbox by building a collection of practices, affirmations, books, music, or activities that uplift and inspire you.*

Turn to these tools whenever you need to reconnect with yourself

MINDFUL MOMENT: Self-love is a lifelong journey, not a destination. Each step you take towards caring for yourself will deepen your connection to who you are. Embrace the process, knowing that you deserve all the love, compassion, and respect you so freely give to others.

Remember you are enough,
just as you are!

Remember you are enough,
just as you are!

CHAPTER TWELVE

THE ART OF LOVING YOU

Remember you are enough, just as you are!

There comes a moment, after all the searching and striving, when you realize that love was never something to be earned or found; it was something to be remembered. Loving yourself is not the end of the journey, but the quiet beginning of every day that follows.

You learn that love is not always soft, and sometimes it asks you to face the shadows you have tried to hide. It asks you to forgive the moments you believed you were unworthy. It asks you to rebuild, again and again, with gentleness and courage.

You start to see that self-love is not a mirror you gaze into, it is the way you speak to yourself in silence, the choices you make when no one is watching, the grace you extend when you falter. It is how you breathe through the chaos and still find beauty in your becoming. Then one day, without realizing it, you stop waiting for someone else to make you whole. You stop searching for validation from others. Instead, you stand tall in your own light, anchored in the truth that you are enough, always have been, always will be.

Loving yourself becomes an art form, a masterpiece that keeps evolving. Some days it is painted in bold colors, radiant and fearless. Other days, it is quiet, unfinished, and tender in its imperfection. Every stroke of the brush matters because every stroke tells a story. Every choice you make to stay, to try, to care for your own heart, is a testament to your becoming.

The art of loving you is not about ultimate perfection. It is about honoring your story, embracing your edges, and allowing love to live in every corner of your body and soul.

So, as you close this chapter, do not forget you are the Art, and you are the Artist.

Remember, the masterpiece is your life still unfolding, still beautiful and yours to create.

Living your life with self-love is a transformative way to approach daily experiences, relationships, and personal growth. It is about embracing who you are, valuing your worth, and showing up for yourself with kindness and compassion. Here are some practical ways to live a life rooted in self-love:

Embrace 1. Prioritize Your Needs

- Self-love means putting your needs first without feeling guilty. This can involve saying no when something does not align with your well-being, protecting your energy, and carving out time for self-care. Trust that taking care of yourself helps you show up better for others.

Embrace 2. Practice Self-Compassion

- Be gentle with yourself, especially during challenging times. Instead of criticizing yourself when you make mistakes, speak to yourself the way you would to a dear friend. Remind yourself that it is okay to be imperfect—growth and learning are part of the journey.

Embrace 3. Set Healthy Boundaries

- Establishing boundaries is a critical aspect of self-love. Know when to say no, when to ask for help, and when to step away from situations that drain you. Boundaries protect your mental, emotional, and physical health, and they show that you respect yourself.

Embrace 4. Accept Your Authenticity

- Living authentically means accepting yourself exactly as you are and not pretending to be someone you are not. Let go of the need to please others and focus on being true to yourself. Celebrate your unique qualities, quirks, and strengths.

Embrace 5. Cultivate Self-Awareness

- Self-love involves understanding who you are, what you need, and what makes you feel fulfilled. Spend time reflecting on your thoughts, emotions, and experiences. Journaling, meditation, and mindfulness are great ways to foster this awareness and strengthen your connection with yourself.

Embrace 6. Focus on Positive Self-Talk

- The way you speak to yourself has a significant impact on your self-esteem. Replace self-criticism with affirmations of love, kindness, and encouragement. Whenever negative thoughts arise, challenge them, and reframe them with compassion and positivity.

Embrace 7. Celebrate Your Achievements

- Take time to acknowledge and celebrate your successes, no matter how small they seem. Each step you take is a victory, and giving yourself credit helps build confidence and reinforce your worth.

Embrace 8. Surround Yourself with Positive Influences

- The people you spend time with should uplift you. Surround yourself with those who support and appreciate you. Let go of toxic relationships or any energy that does not honor your worth. Relationships should nourish and empower you, not drain or diminish your spirit.

Embrace 9. Engage in Activities that Bring You Joy

- Fill your life with things that make you feel happy and fulfilled. Whether it is a creative hobby, nature walks, spending time with loved ones, or diving into a book you have been wanting to read. Prioritize activities that feed your soul.

Embrace 10. Forgive Yourself

- Let go of guilt or regret over past actions. Everyone makes mistakes. The key is to learn from them, forgive yourself, and move forward with compassion. Self-love means releasing any negative emotions attached to past mistakes and choosing to grow from them.

Embrace 11. Embody Self-Care as a Daily Practice

- Self-care is not just about indulging in occasional pampering; it is about integrating small, meaningful practices into your daily routine. Whether it is getting enough sleep, eating nourishing food, exercising, or taking mental breaks, self-care helps keep you balanced and energized.

Embrace 12. Trust Your Intuition

- Learn to trust and follow your inner guidance. When you feel a gut instinct or deep inner knowing about something, honor it. Self-love involves listening to your intuition and trusting yourself to make the right choices.

Embrace 13. Live with Gratitude

- Gratitude is a powerful practice that aligns you with the present moment. By focusing on the things you are thankful for, whether big or small, you cultivate a mindset of abundance and appreciation, which naturally increases self-love.

Embrace 14. Accept Your Flaws and Celebrate Your Growth

- Self-love is not about being perfect but about accepting all parts of yourself. Embrace your flaws as opportunities for growth and self-improvement. Understand that growth is an ongoing journey, and every step you take towards becoming a better version of yourself is an act of self-love.

MINDFUL MOMENT: Self-love requires patience, especially when it comes to healing, growth, and change. Give yourself time to evolve and know that you are always worthy of love at every stage of your life. Do not rush your journey, embrace it as it unfolds.

Living with self-love means creating a life that reflects respect for yourself, your values, and your worth. It is a continuous practice of making choices that honor who you are, even when life gets busy or challenging. This is a simple, structured path for practicing self-love, providing you with practical steps to incorporate into your daily life. Each chapter, "Embrace" and "Soul Work," will empower you to take better care of yourself, deepen your self-worth, and ultimately build a life filled with love and acceptance.

Never broken but becoming!

CHAPTER THIRTEEN

A LOVE LETTER TO ME...

Dear Royal Rhonda,

I see you! Styled in Poppin' colors. Yes, and those heels, you better work it. Rocking that natural hair crown with none other than Phamily Haircare. Lips are all layered in purple lipstick, showing that regalness.

Yes, walking with God's grace!

You were worthy, and you always have been.

Now you know that healing is not a straight line. It is messy, slow, and sometimes lonely. But with every breath, every small win, every act of kindness toward yourself, you have been winning your way back home. I want to thank you for not giving up when you were tired and defeated. For choosing growth when numbness was easier. For learning how to sit with your emotions instead of running from them. It was not weakness but courage. I have watched you become gentler with yourself. More forgiving and more real! I have seen you learn that loving yourself is not a destination but a daily practice. One built on grace, truth, and deep acceptance.

Today, I love you not because you love yourself, but because you have embraced yourself. Flawed, healing, radiant, and most importantly human. You are still becoming, and that is beautiful.

I am proud of how far you have come. I promise to keep showing up for you, not just on good days, but on all the days.

I Love You!!

With all the compassion in the world,

Love is me

The Love I was searching for was always my OWN.
Love Yourself

The author's original photo AI generated

CHAPTER FOURTEEN

TYPES OF LOVE

Love is often confused with kindness or thoughtful gestures, yet to grasp its true philosophical depth, we must first examine its distinct types. The eight classical types of love are rooted in ancient Greek philosophy, each reflecting a unique aspect of human connection. Over time, a few modern interpretations have been added, expanding our understanding of love in today's emotional and cultural landscape (Helm, 2021).

Eros (Romantic/Passionate Love)

Eros is the kind of love that ignites the senses, an intense physical attraction and an undeniable desire that can sweep you off your feet. It often brings the thrilling yet sometimes tumultuous experience of infatuation, marked by emotional highs and lows. This type of love is closely tied to the feeling of falling in love, when everything feels heightened, exhilarating, and all-consuming (Helm, 2021).

Practice:

- Keep the romance alive with intentional time together.
- Express affection with words, songs, or small gifts
- Be emotionally open and physically connected.

Heart work:

Plan surprise date nights when possible and share fantasies through love letters. Remember to compliment your partner lovingly and often.

Philia (Deep Friendship)

Philia represents the affectionate love found between close friends who share loyalty, trust, and common values. It thrives on mutual respect, where each person values the other not for what they can offer, but for who they truly are. This type of love is forged through shared experiences, creating a bond that deepens over time. Unlike fleeting passions, Philia is a stable and enduring love that withstands life's challenges, that remains a constant source of support and understanding (Helm, 2021)

Practice:

- Share honest conversations and support each other's growth.
- Show up consistently and remain confident.
- Engage in mutual activities that build shared memories.

Heart work:

Share stories and talk about life or dreams. Always celebrate each other's wins and never be envious. This deep friendship gives space to be present during difficult times without judgment.

3. Storge (Familial Love)

Storge is the natural, instinctive love and affection between family members, especially between parents and children, or among siblings. It represents the kind of love that is gentle, nurturing, and unconditional, built through shared experiences, trust, and familiarity over time. Unlike passionate or romantic love, Storge is quiet but strong, showing up in daily acts of care, protection, and loyalty (Helm, 2021).

Practice:

- Spend time together regularly.
- Practice patience and forgiveness.
- Create and maintain family traditions.

Heart work:

Commit to Sunday dinners or game nights. Show up and provide emotional support to a sibling or parent. Find time to check in without needing a reason.

4. Ludus (Playful Love)

Ludus is characterized by flirtation, fun, and light-heartedness. It is the kind of love that is playful rather than serious, focusing on enjoyment, teasing, laughter, and the thrill of the moment (Helm, 2021).

Practice:

- Flirt, tease, and laugh together.
- Keep things light and have fun without expectations.

- Do not take yourself too seriously.

Heart work:

Watch a funny movie, share inside jokes, or attend a comedy show. Commit to a spontaneous event like dancing while cooking. Send each other silly memes via text during the day.

5. Mania (Obsessive Love)

This type of love is intense, overwhelming, and often possessive or dependent. It comes from the Greek word *"mania"*, meaning madness or frenzy, and represents a kind of love that is driven by emotional extremes, insecurity, and a fear of loss (Helm, 2021).

Note: While it can feel intense and thrilling, this type of love can become unhealthy if not balanced.

How to Balance (Not Feed) It:

- Practice self-awareness and manage insecurity.
- Build your own identity outside the relationship.
- Seek support or therapy if it becomes controlling or anxious.

Heart work (Healthy Handling):

Communicate when you are feeling jealous, instead of acting on it. Find a healthy space when overwhelmed by emotional dependency.

6. Pragma (Enduring/Committed Love)

This type of love is rooted in long-term commitment, deep understanding, and mutual respect. The term comes from the Greek word *"pragma"*, meaning "practical" or "lasting," and it reflects the kind of love that grows stronger over time through effort, patience, and shared life experiences (Helm, 2021).

Practice:

- Show daily acts of care and respect.
- Create shared goals and grow together.
- Choose each other even during difficult seasons.

Heart work:

Discuss plans like finances or family. Mutual respect is required when supporting each other through illness, stressful times, conflicts, or changes. Never avoid each other during these times!

7. Philautia (Self-Love)

The love we give to ourselves is a vital foundation for all other forms of love. It is not about vanity or arrogance, but about respecting, nurturing, and valuing your own worth and well-being (Helm, 2021).

Practice:

- Practice self-care and set healthy boundaries.
- Speak to yourself kindly and forgive your flaws.
- Pursue things that bring you joy and meaning.

Heart work:

It is okay to say "no" when you are overwhelmed. It is okay to take solo trips and try new things. It is also okay to find time to journal about your wins, growth, or gratitude.

8. Agape (Unconditional/Universal Love)

Agape is the highest and most selfless form of love. A love that is pure, unconditional, and given without expecting anything in return. Rooted in Greek philosophy and later adopted into Christian teachings, Agape represents a universal, compassionate love that extends to all beings (Helm, 2021).

- *1 Corinthians 13:4–8* — Defines the nature of agape love ("Love is patient, love is kind...")
- *John 3:16* — "For God so loved (*agape*) the world that he gave his only Son, that whoever believes in him should have everlasting life."
- *1 John 4:7–8* — "Whoever does not love does not know God, because God is love (*agape*)."

Practice:

- Practice empathy and compassion without expecting return.
- Serve others with kindness.
- Forgive generously and act from love, not fear.

Heart work:

Volunteer and be of service to a stranger. Remember that good deeds do not always require recognition. Love one another despite their imperfections.

CHAPTER FIFTEEN

THEORY OF LOVE

Robert Sternberg's triangular theory of love is a theory that proposes three components of love, which combine in different ways to create eight kinds of love. The three components of love in the triangular theory of love are intimacy, passion, and decision/commitment (Sternberg, 1986).

According to Sternberg, these three components of love combine to create eight kinds of love: nonlove, liking, infatuated love, empty love, romantic love, companionate love, fatuous love, and consummate love (Sternberg, 1986).

The Triangular Theory of Love, proposed by psychologist Robert Sternberg, suggests that love consists of three components: Intimacy (emotional closeness and connectedness), Passion (romantic and physical attraction), and Commitment (decision to maintain the love in the long term).

Sternberg's Triangular Theory of Love | 8 Types of Love

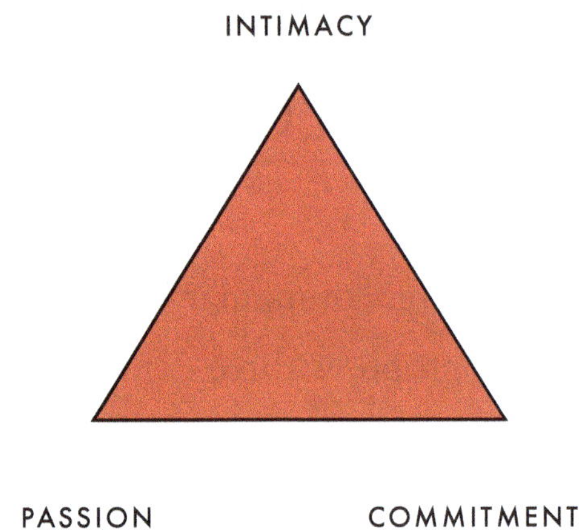

RESOURCES

Mental Health Resources

Disclaimer: Due to the published date of this book, some organizations may no longer be providing services in your state.

988 Suicide and Crisis Lifeline and 988 Textline

BlackLine provides a space for peer support, counseling, witnessing, and affirming the lived experiences of those who are most impacted by systematic oppression with an LGBTQ+ Black femme lens. Call 1-800-604-5841.

Childhelp National Child Abuse Hotline: If you know a child is being hurt or does not feel safe at home, you can call or text 1-800-4-ACHILD (1-800-422-4453)

Domestic Violence Hotline: If you are experiencing domestic violence, looking for resources or information call 1-800-799-7233 or go to thehotline.org to virtually chat with an advocate.

Naseeha is a Mental Health Helpline that answers calls from around the world from Muslims and non-Muslims. Call 1-866-627-3342 for help 24/7.

Physician Support Line is available at 1-888-409-0141 every day from 8 a.m. - 1:00 a.m. ET. Physician Support Line is a national, free, and confidential support line service with over 600 volunteer psychiatrists to provide peer support for other physicians and American medical students.

Project LETS offers a Trans Lifeline to provide support to individuals in crisis or approaching a crisis without police involvement to prevent ongoing systemic disparities for trans populations. Phone: 877-565-8860.

StrongHearts Native Helpline is a confidential and anonymous, culturally appropriate domestic violence and dating violence helpline for Native Americans. Call 1-844-762-8483 every day from 7 a.m. - 10 p.m. CT.

Teen Line provides support, resources, and hope to young people through a hotline of professionally trained teen counselors and outreach programs. Call

800-852-8336 nationwide (6 p.m. - 10 p.m. PST) or text TEEN to 839863 (6 p.m. - 10 p.m. PST).

The Trevor Project is the leading national organization providing crisis intervention and suicide prevention services to lesbian, gay, bisexual, transgender, queer, and questioning youth.

Counselors are available 24/7. Call 1-866- 488-7386, text START to 678-678 or start an online chat at the-trevorproject.org/get-help.

Trans Lifeline call 1-877-565-8860 for the US and 877-330-6366 for Canada. Trans Lifeline's

Hotline is a peer support service run by trans people, for trans and questioning callers.

The Partnership for Drug-free Kids Helpline can be reached at 1-855-378-4373 for support for your family or a loved one struggling with addiction and facing care or treatment challenges. Support is available in English and Spanish, from 9 a.m. - midnight ET on weekdays and noon-5 p.m. ET on weekends.

Veterans Crisis Line connects veterans in crisis and their families and friends through a confidential toll-free hotline, online chat, or text. Open 24/7 call, 1-800-273-8255.

Your Life, Your Voice Hotline The Boys Town National Hotline is open 24 hours a day, 365 days a year to support teens and caregivers with a variety of mental health topics such as anxiety, suicidal ideation, and relationships. The hotline is staffed by trained Boys Town counselors and is accredited by the American Association of Suicidology (AAS). Spanish-speaking counselors and translation services for more than 100 languages are also available. The speech- and hearing-impaired can contact this service at <u>hotline@boystown.org</u>. Call 1-800-448-3000 or text VOICE to 20121 to get started.

ORGANIZATIONS

AAKOMA Project helps youth of color, their families, and their caregivers understand the importance of mental health. *Visit www.aakomaproject.org*

Alliance for a Healthier Generation promotes healthy environments that support whole-child health. Visit *www.healthiergeneration.org*

Anxiety and Depression Association of America (ADAA) is an international nonprofit organization dedicated to the prevention, treatment, and cure of anxiety, depression, OCD, PTSD, and co-occurring disorders through the alignment of science, treatment, and education. *Visit www.adaa.org*

Asian Counseling and Referral Services (ACRS) promotes social justice and the well-being and empowerment of Asian Americans and Pacific Islanders. *Visit www.acrs.org*

Asian Mental Health Collective aspires to make mental health services easily available, approachable, and accessible to Asian communities worldwide. *Visit www.asianmhc.org*

Black Emotional and Mental Health Collective (BEAM) is a national training, movement-building, and grantmaking institution dedicated to the healing, wellness, and liberation of Black and marginalized communities. Visit *www.beam.community*

Black Girls Can Heal is an online community and coaching program dedicated to helping women break the cycles of unavailable partnerships, unhealthy relationships, and feeling not enough to provide via evidence-based and real, actionable tools. Visit *www.blackgirlsheal.org*

Black Men Heal provides access to mental health treatment, psycho-education, and community resources to men of color. Visit *www.blackmenheal.org*

Calathea Wellness helps first-generation Latine professionals embrace their bicultural identity to elevate their confidence, deepen their connections, and amplify their individual and professional fulfillment. Visit *www.calatheawellness.com*

Estoy Aqui offers innovative training programs to providers in the helping professions who want to learn about the socio-cultural aspects of mental health in Latine and Black communities. Visit *www.estoy-aqui.org*

Faces and Voices of Recovery works to change the way addiction and recovery are understood and embraced through advocacy, education, and leadership. *www. facesandvoicesofrecovery.org*

Health Equity Collaborative seeks to eliminate health disparities through a holistic and intersectional approach to healthcare. *healthequitycollaborative.org*

Human Rights Campaign (HRC) is focused on mobilizing those who envision a world strengthened by diversity, where our laws and society treat all people equally, including LGBTQ+ people and those who are multiply marginalized. *hrc.org*

Imi is a series of guides designed with and for LGBTQ+ teens to help explore and affirm their identity. Guides are free, backed by science, and help teens learn practical methods to cope with sexual and gender minority stress in ways that are helpful, relevant, inclusive, and joyful. *imi.guide*

Inclusive Therapists works to make the process of finding a therapist simpler and safer, centering the needs of BIPOC and LGBTQIA2S+ intersections (QTBIPOC). Their mission prioritizes the voices and expressions of neurodivergent and disabled communities of color. *inclusivetherapists.com*

Informed Immigrant is a digital hub and offline network offering the most up-to-date and accessible information and guidance for the undocumented immigrant community. *informedimmigrant.com*

Institute for Muslim Mental Health promotes Muslim Americans' mental health through research, resource development, training, and advocacy. *muslimmentalhealth.com*

Khalil Center is a psychological and spiritual community wellness center advancing the professional practice of psychology rooted in Islamic principles. *khalilcenter.com*

The Kids Mental Health Foundation is driven to create a world where mental health is a vital part of growing up, where children's mental health is as important as their physical health, and where we teach grown-ups the skills to help kids face and manage life's challenges through free resources. *kidsmentalhealth-foundation.org*

Latinx Parenting is a bilingual organization rooted in children's rights, social and racial justice, and anti-racism, the individual and collective practice of non-violence and reparenting, intergenerational and ancestral healing, cultural sustenance, and the active decolonization of oppressive practices in our families. *latinxparenting.org*

Latinx Therapy is a national directory for Latinx Therapists in private practice. Latinx Therapy works to destigmatize mental health in the Latinx community by providing a bilingual podcast, a national directory, and culturally grounded workshops and services. *latinxtherapy.com*

Mental Health Coalition (MHC) was formed to catalyze like-minded communities to work together to destigmatize mental health and empower access to vital resources and necessary support for all, the MHC connects individuals to a range of different resources from Coalition members. *thementalhealthcoalition.org*

The Mental Health Collaborative works to build resilient communities through mental health education and awareness, decreasing stigma, and opening the door to conversations about mental health. They train schools, organizations, and communities in mental health literacy – the foundational education that all of us need to promote our best mental health. *mentalhealthcollaborative.org*

Mixed in America aims to empower the mixed community by facilitating supportive spaces for mixed individuals to explore and unpack their identities. Mixed in America offers services for adults, children, affinity groups, schools, and businesses. Our approach is trauma-informed, holistic, inclusive, and autonomous. *mixedinamerica.org*

Muslim Wellness Foundation utilizes a holistic and spiritually grounded psychological approach to cultivate honest conversations and experiences wherein radical healing, belonging, and growth can flourish. *muslimwellness.com*

Mustard Seed Generation exists to eradicate barriers to mental health that increase life dissatisfaction, family dysfunction, and suicide in the Korean American community. We provide culture-specific training to increase the mental health literacy of Korean American churches, families, and youth. *mustardseedgeneration.org*

Nalgona Positivity Pride is an unconventional eating disorder awareness organization that shines a light on the often-overlooked societal factors that perpetuate unrealistic and oppressive beauty and health standards. NPP offers a vital space for BIPOC individuals to celebrate and embrace their bodies and identities. *nalgonapositivitypride.com*

National Alliance for Eating Disorders works tirelessly to raise awareness; eliminate secrecy and stigma; promote access to care; and support those susceptible to, currently experiencing, and recovering from eating disorders. *allianceforeatingdisorders.com*

National Network for Immigrant and Refugee Rights (NNIRR) works to defend and expand the rights of all immigrants and refugees, regardless of immigration status. *nnirr.org*

National Queer and Trans Therapists of Color advances healing justice by transforming mental health for queer and trans BIPOC individuals. *nqttcn.com*

National School Boards Association (NSBA) works with and through state association members to advocate for equity and excellence in public education through school board leadership. *nsba.org*

The National Parent Teacher Association is a network of millions of families, students, teachers, administrators, and business and community leaders devoted to the educational success of children and the promotion of family engagement in schools. *pta.org.*

Native Hope exists to address the injustice done to Native Americans. We share Native stories, provide educational resources, and assist Native communities. *nativehope.org*

One Sky Center is a National Resource Center for American Indian and Alaska Native health, education, and research. It is dedicated to quality health care across Indian Country. *oneskycenter.org*

Project Heal works to break down systemic, health care, and financial barriers to eating disorder healing. Project Heal's goal is to change the system and, in the meantime, provide lifesaving support to people with eating disorders who the system fails. Learn more at *theprojectheal.org.*

Project LETS builds peer support collectives, leads political education, develops new knowledge and language around mental distress, organizes and advocates for the liberation of our community members globally, and creates innovative, peer-led alternatives to our current mental health system. *projectlets.org*

Q Chat Space provides live, chat-based discussion groups for LGBTQ+ and questioning teens ages 13-19. It is not a forum, and there is no video or audio. Everyone is chatting during the same pre-scheduled time. Q Chat Space chats are facilitated by experienced staff and volunteers from youth programs at LGBTQ+ centers across the U.S. Q Chat Space facilitators are not mental health professionals. *qchatspace.org.*

Radical Mental Health First Aide (RMHFA) is a framework and tool to support you as you make attempts to decenter the medical model from the way you access care, support, love or whatever words you and your community prefer. *connectwithoumou.com/radical-mental-health-first-aide*

Recovery Dharma Online (RDO) is an independent Recovery Dharma community that works together to host safe, inclusive, and reliable Buddhist-inspired recovery meetings. *recoverydharma.online*

Rooted in Radiance empowers historically underinvested communities in Washington, D.C. to prioritize their well-being through innovative, culturally tailored wellness programming. We offer on-site and virtual solutions focused on stress reduction, mental health, and holistic wellness, integrating meditation, breathwork, yoga, and mindfulness to support individuals and teams in achieving peak performance and lasting health. *rootedinradiance.com*

Rural Minds serves as the informed voice for mental health in rural America and provides mental health information and resources. *ruralminds.org*

Teen Talk App is a free, safe, and anonymous space where teens can freely speak to their peers about everyday issues and their overall mental health. Teen Advisors are trained to support their peers through a wide range of experiences, including anxiety, depression, relationships, family issues, school, and more. Teen Advisors are supervised by licensed mental health professionals. *teentalkapp.org*

Therapy for Black Girls is an online space dedicated to encouraging the mental wellness of Black women and girls. *therapyforblackgirls.com*

Therapy for Black Men wants to break the stigma that asking for help is a sign of weakness. With a rapidly growing directory of 608 therapists and 50 coaches throughout the 50 states thus far, Therapy for Black Men provides judgment-free, multiculturally competent care to Black men. *therapyforblackmen.org*

Therapy for Latinx was created to make finding a mental health provider as easy as possible. Search our listings to find therapists who honor who you are, provide services with dignity, and can code-switch like the best of them. *therapyforlatinx.com*

To Write Love on Her Arms (TWLOHA) is a non-profit movement dedicated to presenting hope and finding help for people struggling with depression, addiction, self-injury, and suicide.

TWLOHA exists to encourage, inform, inspire, and invest directly into treatment and recovery. *twloha.com*

TrevorSpace is an affirming international community for LGBTQ young people ages 13-24. TrevorSpace helps young people explore their identities, get advice, find support, and make friends in a moderated community intentionally designed for them. *trevorspace.org*

Well Beings brings together partners from across the country, including youth, families, caregivers, educators, medical and mental health professionals, social service agencies, private foundations, filmmakers, corporations, and media sponsors, to create awareness and resources for better health and well-being. *wellbeings.org*

WithAll aims to serve millions of people with simple, accessible resources that work to reduce the risk of eating disorders through upstream prevention and help people break through practical barriers in pursuing recovery. *withall.org*

Yellow Chair Collective (YCC) provides culturally relevant therapy for Asian Americans. YCC does not simply view therapy as addressing the problem you are facing or the symptom you are experiencing. YCC takes into account who you are as a person first and what is truly important to you. *yellowchaircollective.com*

*****Adapted from Mental Health America*

REFERENCES

Helm, Bennett, "Love", The Stanford Encyclopedia of Philosophy (Fall 2021 Edition), Edward N. Zalta (ed.) Retrieved from https://plato.stanford.edu/entries/love/

Lewis, C. S. (1960). The four loves. Harcourt, Brace.

Liddell, H. G., & Scott, R. (1996). A Greek-English Lexicon (9th ed.). Oxford University Press.

Sternberg, R. J. (1986). A triangular theory of love. Psychological review, 93 (2), 119.

New International Version. (2011). Holy Bible. Biblica.

ABOUT THE
AUTHOR

Rhonda Thomas-Boothe holds a master's degree in psychology with her focus on Organizational Policies and Procedures in the workplace. She is a certified life coach, mentor, Mental Health First Aider, and is a passionate advocate for self-love, healing, and inner growth.

She is the owner of BB Mind over Matter Mentoring & Coaching LLC, where she specializes in helping others cultivate self-worth and emotional resilience. Through her work, she empowers others to rewrite their inner narrative and live from a place of authenticity and compassion.

AFFIRMATIONS

SELF-L♥VE NOTES

SELF-L♥VE NOTES

SELF-L♥VE NOTES

SELF-L♥VE NOTES

SELF-L♥VE NOTES